SIMPLE SOLUTIONS FOR ARTHRITIS

AN ARTHRITIS PATIENT'S PRACTICAL GUIDE TO HEALTH AND HOPE

SIMPLE SOLUTIONS FOR ARTHRITIS

AN ARTHRITIS PATIENT'S PRACTICAL GUIDE TO HEALTH AND HOPE

BY

KIM MANSER HOFMANN

1stBooks – rev. 9/20/00

ABOUT THE BOOK

Read this book for practical guidance on how to improve your day-to-day living with arthritis of any type. You too can learn to live a healthy, active, fulfilling life even with the setbacks of arthritis. Better education, a positive attitude and improved communication are just three areas addressed in this "must read" book. It will let you know you're not alone and it may change your life!

PEOPLE ARE ALREADY TALKING ABOUT THIS BOOK:

"Simple Solutions for Arthritis provides practical tips and techniques for coping with arthritis. Anyone who struggles with the day-to-day challenges of arthritis as well as their friends, family and healthcare professionals, can benefit from Kim Hofmann's insights."

> Valerie Klusas Branch, M.S.
> Director, Arthritis Educator Program
> University of Texas
> Southwestern Medical Center

"One of the biggest losses we who struggle with a chronic illness experience is a sense of losing control over our lives. Kim's book gives us wonderful examples of how we can take back that control by facing the daily challenges of arthritis with renewed faith and an ability to adapt to change in new and unique ways. Simple Solutions for Arthritis is a resource I will recommend to patients and friends alike."

Barbara Butler, M.Ed.
Licensed Professional Counselor
Arthritis Foundation National and North
Texas Volunteer

"This book is a wonderful compilation of strategies for managing arthritis. Within the text of this book are significant short cuts to easy living with arthritis including joint protection and work simplification techniques."

Valerie B. Campbell, OTR
Occupational Therapist
HEALTHSOUTH Plano Rehabilitation Hospital

"An extremely helpful and unique guide to management of problems encountered by rheumatoid arthritis patients. A 'must read'."

Eric R. Hurd, M.D.
Rheumatologist, Arthritis Centers of Texas
Clinical Professor of Internal Medicine
University of Texas
Southwestern Medical Center
U.S. News & World Report, "America's
Best Hospitals/Doctors"

"I feel that this book, <u>Simple Solutions for Arthritis</u>, will be extremely valuable to individuals who have arthritic conditions. Much of what I have done over the past fifteen years in rehabilitation is summarized in this book. There are messages and advice for patients with conditions other than arthritis. In the very first chapter, 'the chairman of the board theory' is presented, which is a realization that the major healthcare provider is none other than the patient.

Nothing could be truer! The doctors, nurses, and therapists are all members of a team, which should be directed by the patient. Often, patients take a passive role when it comes to pain management and healthcare, expecting pills, doctors, or surgery to repair or fix the problem. We all know and realize the pitfalls of taking such a passive approach to medical care. Cures are not often and generally never permanent.

After reading this book, the reader with arthritis should come away with a 'can do' attitude and an increased coping ability regarding medical problems. Some of the ideas in this book are certainly what we call common sense, but it is truly amazing that many of us forget our common sense when we feel bad or are in pain.

I plan on recommending copies of this book to my patients with arthritis as part of my patient education packet.

Simple Solutions for Arthritis is good, easy reading, but entertaining and informative. A person with arthritis will feel empowered after reading this book.

I hope this book becomes required reading for medical residents in the training program of Physical Medicine and Rehabilitation. As rehabilitation specialists we are asked about mobility and activities of daily living. Our patients have all the questions and I believe this book has many of the answers."

Richard R. Jones, M.D., Pharma D.
Medical Director HEALTHSOUTH Plano
Rehabilitation Hospital
Clinical Assistant Professor
University of Texas
Southwestern Medical Center

Past President of DFW Metroplex Physical Medicine and Rehabilitation Society

"This book has some great ideas for people with arthritis as well as family members. It is easy to read with suggestions that work from people that have lived with arthritis. I will suggest it for my patients in the future."

Melissa Peavey, OTR, CHT
Assistant Director
Upper Extremity Specialists
Dallas, Texas

"This book is a great source of ideas for all aspects of life that arthritis can affect. Therapy can be given separately or can be incorporated into daily living."

Corey Ulrich, M.S., PT
Physical Therapist
HEALTHSOUTH Plano Rehabilitation Hospital

"As a business associate and friend of Kim Hofmann, I have seen her in all manner of business, social and private moments. But it wasn't until I read this book that I ever realized how beautifully she copes with her condition while functioning flawlessly in her career and personal life. Kim's tips on coping with arthritis (or any physical, mental or emotional challenge, for that matter) are simple, effective, and like Kim, herself, first rate."

Jan Vernon
Vice President
Human Resources
Cadbury Schweppes Beverages, Americas

DEDICATION

To my immediate family, Arthur, Evan and Caitlin with love; and to my extended family, particularly University of Texas Southwestern Arthritis Educators and our leadership, Peter Lipsky and Valerie Klusas Branch, with deep affection and appreciation.

Kim Manser Hofmann

CONTENTS

ACKNOWLEDGMENTS

I have been blessed with wonderful family and friends and I love them dearly.

Without my parents' early nurturing, I wouldn't have the confidence, positive attitude and determination to deal with arthritis today. My husband, who knew me before the onset of rheumatoid arthritis, has an intimate knowledge of living with this disease on a daily basis. His enduring love has sustained me. Evan, our eldest child, hasn't known me without arthritis. As he said in the videotape, <u>A Positive Journey</u>, "My Mom can do anything that anybody else does, but with some things she needs help." Our daughter, Caitlin, inspired this book. Back in the summer of 1995, when we were floating together on a raft in Lake Michigan, she suggested that I write down all the things that had helped me function with arthritis so that I could help others improve their lives.

My family and friends through the years have been my support group whether they know it or not. They never made me feel limited, although I know accommodations were made along the way. I can't begin to name them all, but a few friends are referenced in the introductions to this book's chapters: Nancy, Patrice, Sheryl and Charlotte and Bill. I'm indebted to Valerie who encouraged this book along for five years. Others have always been there to listen from afar or help nearby when needed—in big and small ways alike. For example, Kathleen and Sue call at the right moment; Julie and Bone also provide support; Jamey listens and challenges; Mom Hofmann prays; in addition to my parents, Carmen cares for Caitlin and Joan for Evan when their help is required; Verna and my church community help with prayers and more; the Yo-Yos encourage and too many other friends to name are my arthritis and prayer warriors. My employer; William Mercer, Incorporated; has provided support during the twenty-three years I have worked with our clients. Last, but not least, I appreciate the book's review team: Dr. Eric Hurd; Dr. Richard Jones; Valerie Branch, M.S.; Melissa Peavey, OTR, CHT and Bob Vernon. You've made a difference in my life and I thank you all. God bless.

AUTHOR'S NOTE

Dear Reader,

Over dinner conversation, a friend said, "Kim, I don't think of you as 'arthritic'." I do have rheumatoid arthritis and for 20 years it has been part of my identity. But it's not my entire identity because I also have a passion for my family, a faith in God, a love of friends, an optimism for life, a sense of humor, a bond with children, a drive for work, an enjoyment for reading, a spirit of volunteerism, an enthusiasm for travel, a fondness for animals, a reverence for nature, an appreciation for the arts, an interest in other cultures and a respect for their beliefs—the list goes on and on. And you may share some of these or have passions of your own.

If you gain a few insights into what can improve your own life, I've accomplished my goal—to share the things that other arthritis patients and I have learned about approaching life with arthritis in a positive, productive way.

Kim Manser Hofmann

Kim Manser Hofmann

FOREWORD

Arthritis is a disease for which there is no cure. Arthritis and related diseases affect over 40 million people in the United States, and it is estimated that that number will increase by 50 percent by the year 2020. This group of diseases involves all ages, all races, and both genders. It is estimated that 50 percent of all people over the age of 55 have osteoarthritis, the most common type of arthritis. Two million people have rheumatoid arthritis, which most commonly affects women in their childbearing years.

I was diagnosed with rheumatoid arthritis 18 years ago while in my early twenties. One of the things that I clearly remember is feeling that no one else was diagnosed with this disease—only my sister and my mother—both of whom had disease progression different than my own. Over the years, I slowly learned how to adapt my lifestyle to this new and constant companion. It was a painful process on a variety of levels. Arthritis affected my employment, my economic status, my social activities and my self-esteem. Fortunately, I realized that knowledge was critical to my well-being and to my long-term outcome. And even though I took every opportunity to learn about the clinical aspects of my disease and its treatment, I could have greatly benefited from practical day-to-day advice that would have made my activities of daily living a bit easier and ease my feelings of isolation.

Kim Hofmann's book, <u>Simple Solutions for Arthritis</u>, provides the reader with relevant, believable suggestions to help one endure the periods of feeling inadequate, depressed, confused, and overwhelmed. Her knowledge is first-hand, since Kim has had rheumatoid arthritis for 20 years, and for the past seven years she has worked as an

Arthritis Educator at the University of Texas Southwestern Medical Center in Dallas, Texas. Kim is one of a team of individuals with arthritis who provides arthritis education to both healthcare professionals and patients at medical centers in the United States and abroad. Her insights and tips are a compilation of her own personal experience and the experiences others have shared with her.

It is comforting to know that others face the same challenges that you encounter, and that those individuals overcame those challenges successfully. Kim's book should be used as a resource for any person with arthritis, whether newly diagnosed or having long-term experience with the disease. She provides useful suggestions on how to cope emotionally with this disease, as well as tools and resources that you can use to educate yourself. Not only is Kim's book helpful for the person with arthritis, but family, friends, and healthcare professionals can gain new ideas on how to help someone with arthritis adapt to changes in lifestyle.

As arthritis becomes more prevalent in our society, individuals will be searching for ways in which to cope. <u>Simple Solutions for Arthritis</u> provides information for either gender at any age. Even though one's body may change through the years due to arthritis, one should still live a productive and meaningful life. This book is a step in understanding and achieving that goal.

Valerie Klusas Branch, M.S.
Director, Arthritis Educator Program
University of Texas
Southwestern Medical Center
Dallas, Texas

CHAPTER 1

INTRODUCTION/HEALTHCARE

"Look to your health; and if you have it, praise God, and value it next to a good conscience; for health is the second blessing that we mortals are capable of; a blessing that money cannot buy." Izaak Walton

Introduction

Before we begin, let me tell you about myself. I led a charmed life until I was diagnosed with rheumatoid arthritis at the age of 27. Besides being on the fast track at work, I was happily married and looking forward to having children. I was an athlete; paddleball, squash, skiing, swimming and volleyball were my sports. We had a wide circle of friends who partied and danced every weekend. We traveled and enjoyed walking around newly discovered

1

cities all day long. Then, with my doctor's news, my life changed; I was devastated. At first I thought life wasn't worth living. However, with a focus on body, mind and spirit, I learned to live a different life. I adjusted my activities and adapted in numerous ways—many of which appear in the chapters ahead. It was not the life I would have chosen, but it is my life and I am living it the best way I can. Today I live a full life—with a career that has not lost it's momentum, a husband, children and friends who support me and a wide range of cultural, religious and charitable activities that sustain me even with the ever-present pain and frustration related to arthritis. I've found that, indeed, "it's a wonderful life." This book is a collection of arthritis wisdom, which I pass on to you. Pass it on to others!

Healthcare

One key to health when dealing with a disease like arthritis is open, honest, two-way communication with your doctor. As my mentor and friend, Valerie Klusas Branch, Director of the Arthritis Educator Program at the University of Texas Southwestern Medical Center at Dallas, says:

I believe in what I call "The Chairman of the Board Theory," which my rheumatologist explained to me. Always think of your body as a profit-making business, and the profits as your health. You aren't an expert in running the business so you hire a Board of Directors. You are the Chairman and the Board members are the health professionals that you employ and look to for advice. As your situation and life changes, you may have to switch members around in that group. But always keep in mind that you're the boss and you're in charge. It's your body; it's your business; it's your health. You are the one in control. You work with the Board as a team, but in the end it's your decision.

1. Don't expect your doctor to "fix" or "cure" you. Doctors are part of the team and medicine is one tool used by the health management team. The team, headed by you, consists of doctors, therapists, nurses, family, friends and social workers.

2. When you're first diagnosed with arthritis, you can suffer from confusion and too much information, especially if your doctor uses terms you don't understand. If you and your doctor don't communicate well, find another doctor (even if you must travel to see him or her). Or, ask for other options if your medical group requires you to choose within its organization.

3. If you are moving or your doctor is no longer in your healthcare plan, ask for the names of other doctors he or she recommends. Then interview prospective doctors before you select a new one. Remember to review the rules of your health plan to see what alternatives you have. The Arthritis Foundation brochure, *Choosing a Health Plan*, can be helpful.

4. When you're feeling great, see your primary doctor and rheumatologist annually to ensure that you are well. It is especially necessary for women who must also remember to have annual "well woman" exams. Have blood work done more often, as needed and recommended by your doctor.

5. If you're depressed because of your illness, treat that too. Your doctor has to know about not only your arthritis symptoms but also related issues.

6. Learn everything you can about your disease. For written material, see The Arthritis Helpbook by Kate Loring and James Fries; Arthritis, A Comprehensive Guide to Understanding Arthritis by James Fries; and *Arthritis Today*, a magazine distributed every other month by The Arthritis Foundation. The Arthritis Foundation website is www.arthritis.org. Publications you can order by calling 800.283.7800 in the U.S. or 404.872.7100 outside of the U.S. include: *Arthritis Answers, Managing Your Pain, Guide to Lab Tests, Managing Your Fatigue,* or *Managing Your Health Care*.

7. Check the Internet for helpful websites by searching the keyword "arthritis" through your Internet search engines. Be careful, though, because the quality of information on the Internet varies greatly. Also be aware that some sites are sponsored by drug or vitamin companies. A few helpful sites I've found are www.ivillage.com's health section, www.drkoop.com's descriptions about arthritis, www.healtheon.com's consumer-oriented medical information or the alternative therapies and nutrition sections of www.selfcare.com. If you're unfamiliar with using the Internet, ask your local librarian to help you.

8. Besides reviewing updates provided through the Arthritis Foundation, look for information on research provided by publications and government/professional groups such as *The New England Journal of Medicine* at www.nejm.org, the National Institutes on Health at www.nih.gov, or the American College of Rheumatology (ACR) at www.rheumatology.org.

9. To help you manage your disease and communicate with your medical advisors, keep a health journal—listing medicines, surgeries, doctor appointments, etc. See the Appendix for a sample under section B.

10. When you are trying to decide which alternative treatment is right for you, consult <u>The Arthritis Foundation's Guide to Alternative Therapies</u>. Tell your doctor about every medicine you take and every alternative therapy in which you participate. Bring all medicine with you to every doctor's visit. To treat you effectively, he or she must know about the alternative approaches as well as the traditional ones that you utilize.

11. Get a 7-day medicine container so that you can remember to take all the medicines you should when you should. You can find them in most drug or grocery stores.

12. Don't self-medicate, because you can run into health problems. Follow the instructions your doctor and pharmacist give you and ask about anything you don't understand.

13. Before you know it, you may have a medicine chest full of prescriptions and over-the-counter drugs. So, at least once a year, do a "spring cleaning" and throw out old prescriptions and drugs whose expiration date has passed. If you can't find the expiration date, follow the rule, "when in doubt, throw it out."

14. Keep a list of questions you want to ask your doctor and take it to your next appointment. Write down his or her responses so that you can refer back to them in the future. See section G of the Appendix for a sample.

15. Use splints for relief of sore joints—hands, wrists, etc. In the case of rheumatoid arthritis, see an occupational therapist for cloth, plastic or silver ring splints. Wear them; the silver rings make attractive jewelry. To find out more, you can contact Silver Ring Splint Company at 800.311.7028 in the U.S. and 804.971.4052 elsewhere or access their Internet site: www.silverringsplint.com.

16. Your occupational or physical therapist can give you advice and catalogues about adaptive aids that will help you with daily living. Examples of adaptive aids are jar openers or pen and pencil grips.

17. Let your dentist know when your jaw hurts because of arthritis in your temporomandibular joint (TMJ). With this knowledge, your dentist can work with you to get the job done as painlessly as possible. Dentists have supports to help you keep your mouth open without exhausting or hurting you unnecessarily.

18. It is common that your medicines won't allow you to drink alcohol anymore because of potential side effects. As an alternative, drink nonalcoholic beer instead of beer with alcohol or cranberry juice instead of wine. It's said that grape juice has a protective effect on the heart. Just be sure to read the information provided with your prescriptions to see if alcoholic drinks are prohibited.

19. To make it easier for you to open your medicines, ask your pharmacist to place non-childproof lids on your prescriptions. Be sure to store all medicines out of reach of children, particularly when they can open yours easily.

20. If your hands ache from arthritis pain and inflammation, ask your doctor to prescribe a paraffin bath. If your doctor can't provide the bath directly, you can order one through a medical supply company or catalogue.

21. If you need surgery, find the best surgeon by asking other patients with arthritis or your doctor for suggestions. Then interview your candidates and ask the tough questions—how many surgeries like this one have you done? What are the potential outcomes? If I were to go for a second opinion, whom would you recommend? Can you give me three patient references that have had the same surgery (only if patient confidentiality is maintained)? Before the interview process, order and read the Arthritis Foundation brochure, *Surgery and Arthritis: What You Need to Know*.

22. Ask both your doctor and pharmacist about each prescription's side effects. Then read the instruction material, which comes with the prescription, and consult your paperback prescription drug guide (or the Arthritis Foundation's *Drug Guide* reprint), which you should be able to find at your local library. If not, try the Internet. The Arthritis Foundation has an easy-to-read guide covering most of the common medications and several drug-specific brochures: *Aspirin and Other NSAIDs, Corticosteroid, Cyclosporine, Gold Treatment, Hydroxychloroquine, Methotrexate, Pencillamine,* and *Sulfasalazine*, for example. Newer brochures, including

13

information on biologicals, are: *Celecoxib (Celebrex), Etanercept (Enbrel)* and *Leflunomide* .

23. Always seek a second opinion for your diagnosis of arthritis and follow-up treatment, including surgeries. Did you know that there are over 100 forms of arthritis, many with varying treatments? The Arthritis Foundation has several brochures online such as: *Fibromyalgia Syndrome, Osteoarthritis, Osteoporosis,* and *Rheumatoid Arthritis.*

"And good news gives health to the bones." Proverbs 15:30

Add your own ideas and e-mail them to kim@solutions4arthritis.com:

CHAPTER 2

COPING

"The bitter and the sweet come from the outside, the hard from within, from one's own effort." Albert Einstein

I was fortunate enough to have an alert internist, who diagnosed me with rheumatoid arthritis and referred me to a rheumatologist in the early stages of the disease. He helped build my underlying foundation for coping by recommending the Arthritis Foundation's six-week Self-Help Course and its Water Exercise Class. At these sessions, I met so many people who unknowingly taught me so much about coping positively with arthritis.

1. Having this disease can make you feel depressed and angry. So, any time you start getting depressed or angry, set a timer for 30 minutes for a "Pity Party." Feel really sorry for yourself for the entire time. When the timer goes off, the party's over!

2. To cheer yourself up on a particularly difficult day, send yourself a bouquet of flowers with the message, "You're terrific! Feel better soon." It will raise your spirits.

3. Write a note to someone else whom you perceive to be worse off than you are. You may feel better about your condition once you consider theirs. In any event, you'll be providing cheer to a soulmate.

4. See a funny movie with a friend, a loved one or alone. Laughter does wonders for your spirits and, in turn, your health. Just read Norman Cousins' classic book tying the holistic approach, including laughter, to health, <u>Anatomy of</u>

<u>an Illness: As Perceived by the Patient</u> (reflections on healing and regeneration).

5. If you can't get to the movies, invite a friend over and ask him or her to bring a rented video. The company may help you feel less isolated.

6. When someone asks, "How are you?" Say, "I'm fantastic" or "I'm great." It sounds silly but it works—you will feel better. Remember the expression, "mind over matter."

7. Avoid negative people; they're contagious. You already feel less than 100 percent; don't let anyone make you feel worse!

8. Join a support group. Sharing your experiences with arthritis will make you realize that you're not alone. If you can't find a group, start one! Also, the Arthritis Foundation has a PALS program (Partners in Arthritis Lay Support) in which trained volunteers are available by phone to support callers who want to speak with others dealing with arthritis. Call your local Arthritis Foundation Chapter to learn more.

9. Write down your own personal goals and review them periodically. This exercise will help you to realize your accomplishments and set your goals for the future. See section D of the Appendix for help in drafting your goals.

10. Watch a helpful videotape ordered from the Arthritis Foundation. In the U.S., call 800.283.7800; outside the U.S., call 404.872.7100. Watching the video may give you the inspiration you need to move forward.

11. Try a writing exercise to handle stress. For three to five days in a row, pick a private place where you won't be disturbed and write for 15 to 30 minutes on the subject of your feelings about having arthritis. Don't worry about your spelling or grammar. This exercise is for your benefit only and you can destroy it when you're done.

12. Take the Arthritis Foundation's Self-Help Course (ASHC) taught by trained volunteers who, in a small group setting, cover such topics as:

-self help principles

-pain control

-relaxation techniques

-exercise

-medications

-nutrition.

The knowledge you will gain and practical tips you will learn can help you cope with the limitations brought on by your pain and fatigue.

13. Don't be too hard on yourself if your memory isn't as good as it used to be. Your forgetfulness may be the result of lack of sleep due to pain, aging, overall fatigue or other factors. Maybe carrying a small notepad (paper or electronic) to jot down reminders would be helpful.

14. Visit your local Arthritis Foundation Chapter. In the U.S., contact 800.283.7800 for the nearest location. If you live in a small town and a Chapter isn't convenient, visit one while you're in a larger city. In most countries, there are local chapters of national rheumatic disease societies.

15. Buy and use an aromatic pillow. The effect can be soothing, especially if you're having trouble sleeping. If you can't afford one, ask for the pillow as a gift from a loved one.

16. If getting up and down is difficult, conserve energy by thinking of several things to do while you're up. The Arthritis Foundation's brochure, *Managing Your Activities*, is a good resource.

17. Keep a personal diary to track trends in your disease. Note the patterns when you feel better or worse. Which activities or attitudes contribute to your health or its decline? Section C of the Appendix will help you with examples of entries that you can make in your diary.

18. Keep a bouquet of fresh flowers at all times on your desk at the office or in a prominent place in your home and admire nature's beauty! The color and fragrance will never fail to cheer you up.

19. Speaking of fragrance, it can raise your spirits. Wear a perfume or cologne that pleases you. Use scented candles too.

20. Switch the television channel from news or drama to comedy. You're dealing with enough adversity already.

21. Read a good book. You will escape into another world...

22. Go to a comedy club and LAUGH! Once again, remind yourself that "laughter is the best medicine."

"Do not let your hearts be troubled and do not be afraid." John 14:27

Add your own ideas and e-mail them to kim@solutions4arthritis.com:

CHAPTER 3

SPIRITUAL AND EMOTIONAL CONSIDERATIONS

"I am certainly convinced that it is one of the greatest impulses of mankind to arrive at something higher than a natural state." James Baldwin

A pivotal point in my own healing occurred after the 1989 San Francisco, California—Loma Prieta earthquake (6.9 on the Richter Scale). Our weekly women's Bible study class in the East Bay met with the Oakland group, which had diminished in size and lost its meeting place as a result of the quake. Many of the women were single heads of household, struggling to keep their jobs and raise their children. Yet they had such an unswerving faith in God and His Goodness. Through their example and the leadership of my teachers, I came to know the love of God in a personal way. God's strength has supported me in times of despair. Whose love and strength supports you?

1. Pray. Pray to God, to Mary, to your guardian angel, to whomever—just pray! More and more healthcare professionals are recognizing a link between faith and healing.

2. Get up and watch the sun rise. The wonder of nature will inspire you to begin your day positively.

3. Listen to an inspirational tape. Be inspired—take your mind off day to day troubles.

4. Build up someone else's self esteem, especially when he or she is down. Enthusiasm is contagious and it will help you too.

5. If you are religious, go to your place of worship or study the Bible, Torah or other prayer book. If not, simply meditate.

6. Wake up to the sound of music—what a pleasant change from the buzz of an alarm clock.

7. Listen to, pray for and provide support to a family member of an arthritis patient—he or she requires help too.

8. Read an inspirational passage every day from the Bible, the Torah, a prayer book, an inspiring novel or a biography.

9. Listen to positive music—classical, gospel or instrumental. Sometimes country & western or blues can make you downright sad.

10. If you can't play an instrument anymore, join a choir or chorus. If you can't sing, act. If you can't act, help out with an orchestra, choir, chorus, or acting group. Did you know the ancient Greeks linked music to health?

11. Acknowledge to yourself that you have arthritis. Then don't be afraid or ashamed to let others know that you have a disease. My experience has shown that most people are interested and supportive.

12. Enjoy what you can do rather than lament over what you can no longer accomplish. Remember that "the glass is half full" (not half-empty) attitude always works.

13. Find the time to watch a spider weave its web. Admire its hard work and beauty. Take a picture and display it in an accessible place to remind you of the wonder of nature.

14. Go for a walk outdoors and celebrate all creations, great and small, in their natural habitat. This activity will give you hope for a better day!

15. For inspiration, think of fellow arthritis patients who continue to be productive—the late Rosalind Russell, the actress and dancer; James Coburn, the actor; Wayne Gretzky, the hockey player; Mike Ditka, the football coach; your own personal heroes. Did you know that Renoir, the great artist, had arthritis? Whom do you know that suffers from arthritis and provides you with inspiration?

"...but we know that suffering produces perseverance; perseverance, character; and character, hope. And hope does not disappoint us, because God has poured out his love into our hearts..." Romans 5:3-5

Add your own ideas and e-mail them to kim@solutions4arthritis.com :

CHAPTER 4

RELATIONSHIPS

"But love is the jewel that wins the world." Moira O'Neill

They say "out of the mouths of babes ...;" how true! When my teenage son, Evan, was about 8 years old, he shared a revelation with my husband, Arthur, and me. "Mom, you love Dad so much that you got a disease named after him—ARTHURITIS!"

1. Give a loved one a hug every day—your spouse, your parents, your child, your friend, your pet, etc. Both of you will feel better.

31

2. Phone a friend or relative who is struggling with arthritis or another problem to encourage him or her. Friends and relatives will encourage you in turn.

3. Read a book aloud with a loved one. Many of us haven't read aloud since we were children and it's just as comforting today.

4. Surround yourself with family and friends. Love is the most potent medicine!

5. If your family members aren't helping and think you're "lazy" or "crazy," tell them otherwise and seek their help. If your plea doesn't work, bring them to your next doctor's appointment to have a family discussion about the disease and effect of arthritis on relationships.

6. Identify and confide in a family member or friend who will listen to you and not judge. Periodically you may need someone you trust with whom to be open and honest.

7. Get a pet—a dog, a cat, a bird or maybe a fish. He or she will be a loyal supporter on good days and bad days.

8. Share love with your significant other as often as possible. It's good for your health—for your body as well as for mind and soul. Take a look at the Arthritis Foundation brochure, *A Guide to Intimacy with Arthritis*. Your significant other will appreciate your love and reciprocate!

9. Help your spouse, your parent, your sibling, your child or your grandchild understand arthritis and your limitations so they don't blame themselves for your pain and aren't afraid of your disease. You must educate your coworkers, too (see Chapter 5, "Work").

10. If your loved one has arthritis, don't forget to take time for yourself and your friends. You need to make time to receive support as well as give it. Don't forget to rest and relax; caregiving is exhausting at times.

11. Family members of arthritis patients must address issues as they arise by talking regularly about such topics as: frustration, fear, anger, depression or dependency. Arthritis adds stress to day-to-day living. So, keep your family communication lines open.

12. Every two or three months, escape for a romantic weekend with your loved one—take a vacation from day to day responsibilities and focus just on each other! It will be

rejuvenating for your health as well as your relationship.

"And now these three remain: faith, hope, and love.

But the greatest of these is love." I Corinthians 13:13

Add your own ideas and e-mail them to kim@solutions4arthritis.com:

CHAPTER 5

WORK

"The world is sown with good; but unless I turn my glad thoughts into practical living and till my own field, I cannot reap a kernel of the good." Helen Keller

Knowing how important my career was to my self-esteem at the age of 27, my rheumatologist advised me to quit work only as a last resort. He encouraged me to reduce my work hours; to take educational and exercise classes; and to rest. His final piece of advice was that I should explain my health situation to my supervisor so that we could work together to discover a mutually acceptable solution. In my case, this approach was both essential and effective.

1. Don't stop working! Find another job if the one you have is too demanding and cannot accommodate your disease. Or, take a leave of absence until you can function productively. Think about getting rehabilitation services and retraining. You may also want to consult the government brochure on Americans with Disabilities (ADA) before you decide what to do. It's available through the Internet at www.ada.handbook.homepage.com.

2. Apply for a flexible work schedule to allow time for rest if you are experiencing fatigue. Fatigue is a common occurrence for people with arthritis. More organizations are offering flexible work schedules; see your human resources or personnel representative to explore the possibilities at your workplace.

3. If you can no longer complete an aspect of your work without damaging your joints, talk to your supervisor about reallocating work among your coworkers. Perhaps you can take on additional tasks, which are less physically strenuous. Remember that you may be protected under the ADA. Consult your lawyer if your employer is not receptive to your needs and concerns.

4. Ask your rheumatologist if he or she can use you to teach others—to call newly diagnosed patients or to demonstrate and discuss changes in your body and life with medical students.

5. If your hands or wrists are affected by arthritis, shaking hands can be painful: Hug, if it's appropriate. Say your hand hurts from arthritis and, if you can't shake, shake the forearm. Or, try this approach: push in as far as possible at the web between the thumb and index finger, grab the palm and shake gently and quickly.

6. If you have a child with arthritis, talk to his or her teachers about your child's situation. Teachers who are educated about arthritis can become advocates for your child. For advice about time off from work when your child or spouse has arthritis, consult the government publication on the Family Medical Leave Act which you can find through the Internet at:

www.dol.gov/dol/esa/fmla.htm.

7. Move around so your joints that are affected by arthritis won't tend to stiffen. While at work, take a walk around the office occasionally to remain more productive.

8. If you're traveling for work, walk up and down the train or plane aisles or schedule road trip stops so that you can get out and stretch your sore joints.

9. Ask for adaptive devices at work—a higher chair, an automatic pencil sharpener and stapler or a letter opener (or ask someone to open your mail and packages).

10. When you're struggling with some of your current job functions, talk to your supervisor about continuing to build skills in alternate ways so as to add value at your workplace.

11. For helpful information, order the Arthritis Foundation brochures, *Arthritis and Employment*, *Arthritis in the Workplace* and *Managing Your Stress*. You can place your order on the Internet through the Foundations's website: www.arthritis.org.

12. If you need someone to talk to about work-related or other problems, many companies offer a service to employees called Employee Assistance Programs (EAP). By calling a toll-free number on a confidential basis, a counselor will talk through your issues with you and possibly refer you on to other resources for assistance. Ask your human resource or personnel department if this benefit is available to you. Some EAPs today offer referral services for alternative medicine providers.

13. In addition to your work, volunteer for something…anything. Helping others in your community or your place of worship will help you in turn. Arts, health, political and other special interest groups are always looking for volunteers. Did you know the Arthritis Foundation has a program in which people with arthritis help others? Contact your local chapter.

14. Volunteer to help with your children's activities. If you can't coach a team, make phone calls or schedule snacks. If you can't volunteer in the classroom, ask the teacher what you can do outside the classroom. For example, you can prepare materials for class, provide transportation or organize a committee.

"All hard work brings a profit." Proverbs 14:23

Add your own ideas and e-mail them to kim@solutions4arthritis.com:

CHAPTER 6

PLAY

"It is a happy talent to know how to play." Ralph Waldo Emerson

I was complaining about not being able to play paddleball or squash anymore. My friend (the woman who introduced me to my husband) responded, "So, you can't play sports anymore. Big deal! There's more to life than sports." She was right, and it was the jolt I needed to get back to priorities.

1. Don't give up going to an amusement park, a large indoor mall, the arboretum, the zoo or a park—borrow or rent a wheelchair and go with a friend. You'll have fun!

2. If you can no longer play the piano, try a keyboard that requires a lighter touch. The joy that music brings is healing!

3. If you're a golfer, read the Arthritis Foundation's brochure, *Golf and Arthritis*. It's full of helpful advice so that you might be able to continue playing.

4. If you can't play sports anymore because of limitations brought on by arthritis, don't give it up; watch it on television, read about it in the paper, see movies about "our sport" and take out books and magazines from the library about famous sportsmen and women. Or try an alternative, less invasive sport, like swimming or bike riding.

5. Go fishing. If you can't handle deep sea or bass fishing anymore because of physical changes, switch to crappie or perch fishing, which requires less strength.

6. Play with your children or grandchildren in a pool, where it's possible to lift, carry, hug and throw them effortlessly with the support of the water. You will be able to do things underwater that you can't do otherwise.

7. When you've asked people over for dinner and you have a flare-up, reschedule the evening or keep the dinner simple. Order delivered pizza or take-out Chinese and serve ice cream, a frozen pie or ice cream cake for dessert.

8. Play with children as often as you can—your children, grandchildren and nieces and nephews, or the children of your friends or neighbors. And don't forget your pets!

Children and pets will love your attention and you will benefit as well from the joy that they bring to you.

9. Take a vacation near an ocean, a lake or a stream. The sight and sound of water is therapeutic. You can even find CDs or tapes of nature's sounds, such as those of crashing waves or a babbling brook, if you can't travel to be near them.

10. When a flare-up interferes with social plans, offer alternative, more restful activities, such as going on a picnic, where you can take a nap while your companions play a game or you can take a stroll or a hike. Or suggest going to a movie, where you can sit and relax and enjoy what's happening on the big screen.

11. If you're at a social gathering and feeling tired from the pain of arthritis, let your guests know that you occasionally must leave the festivities to rest. You might tell them, "Don't worry, carry on! I'll be back soon, reenergized. Wake me up in 20 minutes."

12. Keep up with your favorite hobbies as long as you can, e.g., gardening, hunting or quilting. But when you can no longer actively participate, attend events or read publications that focus on your hobbies. See the Arthritis Foundation brochure, *Gardening and Arthritis*.

13. If you enjoy music or art, attend concerts and art shows. These activities are less strenuous, revitalizing and often free.

"David would take his harp and play." I Saul 16:23

Add your own ideas and e-mail them to kim@solutions4arthritis.com:

CHAPTER 7

EXERCISE, WELLNESS AND EDUCATION

"The wise for cure on exercise depend." John Dryden

A coworker was diagnosed with breast cancer and faced decisions about her course of treatment. She remarked, "One thing that you have taught me, Kim, is to learn all that you possibly can about your disease." I'm pleased to report that years later she is cancer-free, enjoying life and helping others learn how to stay well physically and emotionally with her disease.

1. Take a walk with someone who understands your pace. Then you won't feel like you're slow when you're exercising.

2. Take a nap. It will revitalize you and give you energy for your next activity.

3. Ride a bike...even if it's stationary. If you can't use hand brakes because of arthritis in your hands, ride a bike with foot brakes. Many people with arthritis can no longer run, jog, do aerobics, use exercise equipment or lift weights because of the pain or wear and tear on their joints. Biking is a great alternative in many cases. So is swimming!

4. Start an exercise program and follow it at least three times a week. See the Arthritis Foundation brochure, *Exercise and Your Arthritis.*

5. Good health involves every aspect of your being—your mind, your soul and your body. So, exercise all of them as often as possible (see Chapter 3, "Spiritual and Emotional Considerations").

6. Exercise with a friend—it's more fun and it will motivate you to maintain your regimen. You might want to use one of the Arthritis Foundation videotapes available by calling 800.283.7800 in the U.S. and 404.872.7100 elsewhere.

7. Follow the "two hour rule." If you still experience pain two hours after exercising, stop the activity and consult with your doctor.

8. If you neglect your exercise program, don't beat yourself up—start again. You already feel guilty about not exercising, so why add to the guilt?

9. Swimming is the best exercise—join the YMCA, YWCA or a local health club. See the Arthritis Foundation brochure, *Water Exercise: Pools, Spas and Arthritis.*

10. Review your diet for improvements. Drink lots of water and reduce sugar, fat, salt and caffeine in an effort to improve your overall health. See the Arthritis Foundation brochure, *Diet and Arthritis.*

11. If you're unsure of your diet, consult a nutritionist, do research on the Internet or visit your library to obtain information. Keep a diary until good eating becomes a way of life for you. See the Appendix for "Your Daily Activities Diary."

12. Treat yourself to fat-free frozen yogurt often. It tastes good and doesn't have the fat content of ice cream.

13. Join the Arthritis Foundation. For a small donation, you'll receive a magazine and updates on local resources for exercise, nutrition and all sorts of other information and education.

14. Enroll in a water exercise class. Your local YMCA, YWCA or rehabilitation center may sponsor one. With the water's support of your joints, you'll be able to move more easily, maintain your flexibility longer and improve your health, all at the same time!

15. Don't forget that the Arthritis Foundation has a brochure, *Water Exercise*, and a videotape, *PEP–Pool Exercise Program*, which you can order if you'd like to do the exercises on your own or with a friend instead of in a group setting. They also sponsor a program taught by trained volunteers and conducted in an indoor pool with a water temperature of 83-88 degrees Fahrenheit. This program is called the Arthritis Foundation Aquatic Program (AFAP).

16. Try yoga; an exercise for the body, mind and emotions. It's energizing and not too strenuous. Even if you can't achieve all the yoga positions, participate as much as you can and also benefit from the serenity that meditation provides.

17. Tai chi, a Chinese health-giving form of movement therapy, is also worth a try. Look into the programs offered by your local recreation, senior citizen or worship center.

18. If you're overweight, start a weight-reduction plan of diet and exercise. Extra weight hurts your joints.

19. So that he or she can learn more about the disease and its treatments, give someone whom you know and who has arthritis a membership to the Arthritis Foundation. The accompanying free subscription to *Arthritis Today* offers ideas on exercise and nutrition.

20. If your medical clinic, local hospital or rehabilitation center has an educational series for arthritis patients, attend it and bring along a family member or friend. Nutrition classes may be helpful also and are offered in health, fitness and recreational facilities.

21. Stand up straight! When in pain, you will tend to slouch. Good posture will make you feel and look better.

22. Your body may change, but remember that other aspects of you will not ... your mind, your soul, and your heart, for example. See Chapter 3, "Spiritual and Emotional Considerations."

23. Exercise at your own level and pace—if you can't manage a cross-country ski machine, move to a treadmill. If you can't handle a treadmill, what about a stationary bicycle? Check the paper for used equipment! See the Arthritis Foundation brochure, *Walking and Arthritis*.

24. Don't forget to address any special needs that you may have. For example, order one of the following Arthritis Foundation brochures if it relates to you, a loved one or even a student (if you're a teacher): *Arthritis and Pregnancy, Arthritis and Children, Decision Making for Teenagers with Arthritis, Understanding Arthritis in*

African-Americans, or *When Your Student Has Arthritis: A Guide for Teachers.* Several brochures are available in Spanish as well as English.

"Moses was educated in all the wisdom." Acts 7:22

Add your own ideas and e-mail them to kim@solutions4arthritis.com:

CHAPTER 8

DAILY LIVING

"He who limps is still walking." Stankislaw Lec

As a friend and I discussed the challenges that a rheumatoid faces in coping with day to day activities, he observed, "Normal people just lead simpler lives. They don't have to worry about how they're going to get all the jars, cans or bags open to prepare a meal. They don't have to think of all the things that they can accomplish while they're up because getting up and down or even walking is so painful. Life just isn't so simple anymore, but you still have to live it."

1. Because food preparation can be painful and difficult if your hands and wrists are affected by arthritis, buy easy-to-prepare foods. Pre-cut salads and fruit, frozen lasagna and prepared spaghetti sauce are simple to make and taste good, too. A helpful guide from the Arthritis Foundation is *Managing Your Activities*.

2. If you're cooking homemade spaghetti sauce, make it in large quantities and freeze meal-size portions in separate containers. Defrost, heat, cook up some pasta and voila!— you have an easy meal. If you require help chopping, use a food processor or ask someone to assist.

3. A number of restaurants in larger communities will deliver to your home, either through a service or independently. Use them as often as you need them.

4. Read a story to a child rather than playing ball. He or she will be spending time with you. After all, the most important aspect is spending time with each other, not the activity itself.

5. Ask your family to keep the lids on jars loose so that you can open them—but watch out, don't lift them by the lid once they've been opened! You can also purchase jar openers at your local stores or through catalogues that feature adaptive devices for the physically challenged.

6. Put on sunscreen and enjoy the sun. Be careful, though, because sun is not recommended for those with lupus or patients taking certain medicines that sensitize the skin. Check with your doctor.

7. If writing out checks to pay bills is painful, have someone help you or pay the bills electronically on your home computer.

8. Buy an arthritis or easy-to-prepare cookbook or check one out from the library. Many magazines and newspapers are helpful too. <u>Bon Appetit</u> has a "Too Busy to Cook" section.

9. Obtain a handicapped tag or license plate. See your doctor and state's motor vehicle department about an application. You need one!

10. Because arthritis can be unpredictable, keep a two-part "to do" list—one for good days, one for bad. For example, fold laundry on good days and write notes on bad. See the Appendix for samples under sections E and F.

11. If you can't carry your trash because your hands are affected by arthritis, use a child's red wagon to bring trash out to the curb or ask a family member or neighbor.

12. If you have arthritis involvement in your temporomandibular joint (TMJ), avoid hard-crusted rolls, bagels and French bread, which are particularly difficult to chew.

13. If you have lost handgrip strength and can't maneuver doorknobs easily, switch doorknobs to door levers or cover knobs with rubber covers. Even rubber bands will do the trick! You can find door levers or covers at a hardware or home improvement store.

14. If you can't sit up and read a book without discomfort, take out an audiotape from the library or rent one from a local shop. You can also obtain them through the Internet at such sites as www.amazon.com, www.barnesandnoble.com, or www.booksontape.com or by mail by calling 800.88.BOOKS in the U.S.

15. Replace your old utensils with thick, black, rubber-handled utensils. They're arthritis-friendly if you experience hand pain or if you have lost flexibility in your hands.

16. Gallon or two litre size beverage containers are heavy and difficult to handle when your hands hurt. Buy smaller, easier to manage containers of milk, water and juice.

17. When you're at a restaurant and can't easily maneuver the eating utensils because of pain, swelling or stiffness in your hands and wrists, order a sandwich that is less troublesome to eat!

18. Use a down comforter rather than a blanket for warmth—it puts less pressure on your joints! If your feet hurt, a heavy blanket or bedspread can cause additional pain.

19. There are times when you need all the help you can get. Teach your children to care for themselves early and often! They can make their own beds, fold laundry, prepare a simple breakfast or lunch, load and unload the dishwasher, take out the garbage, walk the dog—you name it and they can do it!

20. You can feel helpless to complete simple tasks when you're not at home unless you have a portable "tool kit."

Carry the tools you need...a pair of pliers to turn the car key ignition or collapsible scissors to open snack bags. I often rely on my keychain, which has a miniature Swiss Army knife!

21. Part of coping with arthritis is protecting your joints from further debilitation. Whenever possible, use your larger joints, e.g., nestle a bag in your forearm, instead of carrying a bag with your hand and fingers or wrists.

22. To protect your joints from damage, switch your handbag or briefcase to a smaller version and clean out the nonessentials—they only add weight!

23. Ask someone to help you reorganize your kitchen for easy handling. It can change your life!

24. When you're looking for a new place to live, make sure everything you will need is on the first floor: bath, toilet and bed. Just as people with young children in their homes "child proof" their houses, make your home "arthritis friendly."

25. If you need your gutters cleaned or other heavy work done and can't do it yourself, ask a friend or neighbor. He or she wants to help, so provide that opportunity. Return the favor with a meal or a gift and a note of thanks.

26. Use thick pens and pencils (or place foam tubing around the ones you have) for easier handling. Dr. Grip makes ballpoints and mechanical pencils that are easier to use.

27. If you are having difficulty with your hands, ask for lighter-weight glasses and cups at restaurants. Lighter-weight mugs are easier to hold than the delicate handles on coffee and teacups. And ask your server to pour from a pitcher for you!

28. Housekeeping can be tiring, especially if you don't have much energy. Put memorabilia behind glass in a hutch or under glass in a glass-topped table. You'll have less to dust.

29. If writing is difficult for you, have holiday cards pre-printed with your name and enclose a newsy letter that you have copied for friends. Someone can help you address envelopes or you can print labels on your home computer. The same applies to baby announcements or change of address cards.

30. Place a rubber fingertip cover used for sorting paper on your fingers when you are doing needlepoint. You'll have better control of the needle when you're sewing.

31. Plastic grocery bags are difficult if your hands or wrists hurt, so slide the handle up to your forearm. Don't forget to ask for assistance in loading the bags in your car. Or, ask your grocery store if they deliver. If the cost is affordable, treat yourself.

32. More and more grocery store chains are offering online ordering and delivery for a reasonable fee. See www.GroceryWorks.com, www.HomeGrocer.com, or www.Streamline.com as examples and ask about this service if your local stores currently don't provide it. If they don't, lobby for it!

33. If you enjoy crocheting, ask someone to enhance your crochet hook with a large cork to make it easier to grasp.

34. Give your thumbs a rest. Try using the palms of your hands to carry objects such as trays. Using two hands can also make carrying objects less stressful on your hands. You have better control of the object and the weight is evenly distributed.

"Anyone who is among the living has hope."
Ecclesiastes 9:4

Add your own ideas and e-mail them to kim@solutions4arthritis.com:

CHAPTER 9

TRAVEL

"To forget pain is to be painless; to forget care is to be rid of it; to go abroad is to accomplish both." Mark Twain

One passion my husband and I share is travel. Every other year or so, we try to visit a place we've never been before. We even have a "competition" about which one of us will have visited all 50 states first! (He's ahead at 48. I'm close behind at 46.) On a recent trip to Paris and Provence, France, one part of our tour required walking down a long, steep incline to get to a quaint restaurant by the sea. Rather than being thankful for a cab driver who was willing to take me to the restaurant, I regretted not being able to walk there like everyone else in our group. My husband responded, "Look at the bright side. You'll get to the restaurant first and can pick out the best seat in the house. Anyway, you have the cutest limp of anyone I know." Besides making me laugh, his comments got me back on track for the rest of the tour.

1. Make sure your hotel provides key cards rather than keys; they're easier to use when your hands hurt or are stiff.

2. The next car you buy should be easy to maneuver; easy to get in and out of; and have automatic shifting, windows, defroster, gas cap and trunk release. These features will make driving more enjoyable.

3. If you prefer carry-on luggage, use a small suitcase with wheels instead of a garment bag. When purchasing the suitcase, look for one with the retractable handle on the broad side, not the narrow side. It will be more stable.

4. If you have arthritis in your neck (cervical spine involvement) and your neck movement is limited, take an inflatable neck pillow with you for long plane, train, bus or car rides.

5. During airplane travel, use one of the small pillows provided on airplanes to support your lower back. You'll be more comfortable traveling and arrive at your destination with less back discomfort.

6. If you have trouble opening a can, bottle or snack bag while on a plane trip, ask the flight attendant for help. He or she can open it easily for you. You should also ask the flight attendant to cut up the meat served with your entrée.

7. Call ahead to arrange to have a wheelchair or cart for the handicapped meet you at your arrival gate at the airport. The long walk between gates can be troublesome if your feet, knees or hips are hurting.

8. Don't be afraid to ask for help while traveling. Most travel industry employees are service oriented and are glad to assist you.

9. Travel light. Only pack the items that you will need and be sure to include a bathing suit in case your hotel has a whirlpool or pool. The water exercise and rest will be invigorating.

10. Request an aisle seat on a plane, train or bus. You will be able to get up and walk around during your trip and minimize swelling and stiffness.

11. When you travel, get up and stretch whenever you can—you'll feel better.

12. Drink lots of water when you're on a flight. Arthritis may make you parched and dehydration only worsens the situation.

13. Because of the dehydration factor, don't wear contact lenses on a long flight. Wear your glasses, carry eye drops, and use them as needed.

14. Request a hotel room specially fitted for the disabled.

15. If your knees or hips are affected by arthritis, ask for a raised toilet seat when you make reservations at your hotel as an alternative if a room for a disabled person is not available.

16. If you can't manage the bath or shower handles in a hotel room because your hands aren't flexible, ask for adaptive devices when you make reservations or when you arrive.

17. When you can't open a bottle of shampoo or a tube of toothpaste, call the front desk for assistance. In the alternative, carry a rubber band or user friendly opening device.

18. Always bring your medicine labels with you when you travel so you can get refills at another pharmacy. Also, always take an extra supply of medicine with you in case you decide to extend your stay.

19. Make sure your hotel room is near the elevator. If it isn't, have your room switched.

20. Always carry a folding chair as well as a blanket in your car trunk. If you want to go to the beach or a park, others can sit on the blanket and you can get up and down easier from the chair.

21. A folding chair is useful if you have to stand on line for any length of time.

"...door was always open to the traveler." Job 31:32

Add your own ideas and e-mail them to kim@solutions4arthritis.com:

CHAPTER 10

PERSONAL CARE

"Joy and sorrow, beauty and deformity, equally pass away." Sa'di

There will be days when you will feel downright lousy—and look it! When I experience one of those days, I wear an outfit that I particularly like and know is flattering. For example, whenever I wear a royal blue dress, people comment, "What a great dress! That color looks good on you." It instantly lifts my spirits. What color makes you feel better?

1. When you can't manage it yourself, have a manicure/pedicure—either by a professional or a friend.

2. Have a massage to work out stressed joints and muscles. Massage schools sometimes offer discounts to seniors and individuals who are disabled. If you can't afford a full massage, just have a facial or foot reflexology—they're less expensive and still great for men and women alike.

3. Go to a body and bath shop and buy fragrant oils and creams to use when your skin is dry or itchy. Sensitive skin is a common condition of arthritis or may be a side effect from the drugs you take.

4. Wear bright colors—they make you feel good and look great!

5. Funky socks are fun too and will lift your spirits!

6. Get a new hairstyle—one that's easy to maintain. The change will be good for you and make your morning routine easier if morning stiffness is a problem for you.

7. When your feet hurt, wear comfortable shoes ... SAS (San Antonio, TX), Clark's (England), ECCO (Denmark), Birkenstock (Germany), Pedors (www.pedors.com), etc.

8. Often those with arthritis find it challenging to dress— oh, those zippers and buttons! Buy easy-to-wear clothes with big buttons in the front, with no buttons or zippers in back, and overhead shirts and sweaters in larger sizes than you normally wear. Or, contact J.C. Penney for their *Special Needs* catalogue of easy-to-wear fashions with Velcro closings.

9. So what if you can't take baths anymore because you can't get in and out of the tub? Instead, enjoy long, leisurely showers alone or with the one you love!

10. If your neck (cervical spine) is limited in motion, ask your hairdresser to be gentle when washing your hair over a sink to avoid injury or pain.

11. When you're having difficulty washing your hair because you can't raise your arms, ask a friend or relative over to do it for you, or treat yourself to a trip to the salon.

12. Consider a large body pillow to help you sleep or hug the one you love. Be more comfortable as you try to doze off.

13. Wear Dr. Scholl's sneakers with Velcro closings, especially when your hands hurt and you find tying your shoelaces too difficult.

14. Find a way to purchase a hot tub. What a great way to start and end the day! Look for moving sales and buy a used tub. See the Arthritis website, www.arthritis.org, for articles about spas and their use. Obtain a doctor's prescription and you may not have to pay sales tax or value added tax (VAT).

15. If your eyes are dry, use eye drops without the redness reduction feature. Your eyes will be refreshed afterwards.

16. Buy or rent a raised toilet seat from a medical supply shop or service if your hips and knees bother you when getting up and down from the toilet.

17. Go through your closet and give away to charity any clothes and shoes that you can no longer wear. Have the charity pick them up at your door. Or have a garage sale and use the proceeds to finance a new arthritis friendly wardrobe-shopping spree. In bright colors, of course!

18. Men—select easy to put on shoes and socks. Women—instead of panty hose, wear long skirts with knee or thigh highs or skip skirts altogether and wear slacks.

19. Men—if you can't handle razors anymore because of arthritis in your hands, get an electric one. Women—shaving your legs can be replaced by waxing or hair removal lotions.

20. Take note of what color you're wearing when people compliment you on your attire and wear it more often. You'll feel better!

21. Use the disposable dental floss holders when your hands hurt. They're easier to manage than dental floss.

22. Instead of squeezing the toothpaste tube with your sore fingers, use your forearm.

23. Rather than aerosol hairspray, buy the easy-to-use pump spray.

"Charm is deceptive, and beauty is fleeting." Proverbs 31:30

Add your own ideas and e-mail them to kim@solutions4arthritis.com:

CHAPTER 11

ATTITUDE AND ENVIRONMENT

"Men are like plants: the goodness and flavour of the fruit proceeds from the peculiar soil and exposition in which they grow." Michel Guillaume Jean De Crevecoeur

As an Arthritis Educator, I have traveled to university medical centers to teach the joint exam to other patients with arthritis. They, in turn, teach the exam to physicians-in-training. On a trip to Harvard, I met a young man who talked to me about the supportive relationship that he and his wife, a person with arthritis, experienced. At one point he even quoted the late Jim Valvano, the former North Carolina State NCAA Basketball championship coach, talking about his experience with chronic disease: "Cancer can take away all my physical abilities, but it cannot touch my mind, it cannot touch my heart, and it cannot touch my soul." The same can be said of arthritis.

1. Set your goals every year and review them monthly. When reality knocks you down, accomplishing goals will bring you back up. Section D of the Appendix has some examples to help you set your goals.

2. Determine what your gifts are and share them with others. You may not be physically strong, but if you are emotionally strong, support others! If you're a good listener, let others talk; if you're a gifted speaker, volunteer to give presentations to groups about arthritis; if you're a humorist or storyteller, make people laugh, etc.

3. Place a wind chime above your back door. The sound is soothing and delightful.

4. Hang up a whimsical mobile someplace where you can admire its gentle flow in the breeze. The distraction will please you.

5. Buy a picture, painting or poster that makes you feel good and place it where you'll see it often.

6. Surround yourself with photos of family and friends. They'll comfort you by reminding you of all for which you must be thankful.

7. Ask for help when you need it. Although it's hard to do at first, it will become easier each time that people respond positively and they will, more often than not. People often want to help. You need to tell them how they can help and when not to assist.

8. Tell people about your limitations. They will not know unless you tell them.

9. Choose to be happy, healthy and productive every day. Remember Dale Carnegie said: "Act enthusiastic and you'll be enthusiastic!"

10. Keep your sense of humor. When a coworker is limping from too much exercise, jokingly say that he or she is mimicking your gait. Or tell everyone that your boss makes you "run around at work" when sneakers are the only shoes your feet will tolerate! As you open up about your disease, others will feel more comfortable speaking with you on the subject of arthritis.

11. Don't let your pain allow you to forget to say a simple "thank you" to those who help you—healthcare workers, family members, friends or helpful strangers. They'll appreciate it and perhaps be more inclined to help you and others again.

12. Even if you don't appear (to the untrained eye) to have physical limitations, ask for help unapologetically at the grocery store—you need it! This concept may be difficult at first but, if someone gives you a hard time about it, educate him or her on your circumstances. When this situation has occurred, I have found that the person has been apologetic for his or her actions.

13. Reevaluate the colors in your home. If you need cheering up, think of painting a room yellow. If a room is "hot" and you need calm, paint it blue or green. Instead of using flat white paint, think of mixing in some pink or orange to add a little warmth. As research demonstrates, colors do affect your mood.

14. Stop by the library or use the Internet to find out about Feng Shui, the Chinese art and science of creating a healthy and harmonious environment. You may find Feng Shui helpful to your attitude toward life.

15. Don't let it bother you if someone thoughtlessly comments on changes to your appearance resulting from your disease and medications. Most people will be embarrassed if you tell them the reason for the change. Very few people will be rude and insensitive and you won't be able to reach them anyway. As my friend from New Jersey says, "forget about it!"

16. Add goldfish in a small bowl or an aquarium with tropical fish to your home or office; fish are so relaxing to watch! Watching fish will also reduce your stress level. In addition to Goldie, our goldfish won at a school carnival game and currently residing on our kitchen counter, I have Henri Matisse's painting, *Goldfish*, hanging on my wall at work.

17. Look for higher than normal couches and chairs. They're easier to get in and out of if your knees and hips are limited by arthritis.

"Be made new in the attitude of your minds."
Ephesians 4:23

Add your own ideas and e-mail them to kim@solutions4arthritis.com:

<u>APPENDIX</u>

Kim Manser Hofmann

A. YOUR OWN NOTES

Kim Manser Hofmann

B. YOUR OWN HEALTH JOURNAL

(Bring this to your health appointments for reference)

Current Medicines I'm Taking:

Name	How Much?	How Often?	Price

Doctors/Nurses:

Name	Address	Phone No.	Appts.	Cost

Physical/Occupational Therapists:

Name	Address	Phone No.	Appts.	Cost

Nutritionist:

Name   Address   Phone No.   Appts.   Cost

Alternative Therapies, e.g., Massage, Acupuncture, Biofeedback, Aromatherapy

Name   Address   Phone No.   Appts.   Cost

Exercise Program:

What?   How Often?   What Duration?   Any Pain After Two Hours? If so, stop.

<u>Surgeries:</u>

<u>What?</u>   <u>When?</u>   <u>Drs.</u>   <u>Results</u>   <u>Follow-up</u>   <u>Cost</u>

<u>Blood Tests, Eye Exams, If Needed Due To Medicines I'm Taking:</u>

<u>What?</u>   <u>When?</u>   <u>Results</u>   <u>Cost</u>

<u>What Makes Me Feel Better? (do more of):</u>

<u>What Makes Me Feel Worse? (do less of):</u>

Kim Manser Hofmann

C. YOUR DAILY ACTIVITIES DIARY

Level of Pain/Stiffness/Fatigue

Day   Time   Description

Exercise Routine

Follow the "two hour rule." If you hurt two hours following exercise, stop your routine until you consult with a physician.

Exercise   When?   How Long?   Observations

Day 1

Day 2

Day 3

Day 4

Day 5

Day 6

Day 7

Diet

	Breakfast	Lunch	Dinner	Snacks	Notes
Day 1					
Day 2					
Day 3					
Day 4					
Day 5					
Day 6					
Day 7					

Noticeable Changes

Physical findings or things I could do six months ago that I can't do today without difficulty:

D. YOUR PERSONAL GOALS

Develop your goals by answering such questions as:

-What is important to me?

-What do I want to accomplish in the next six months, year,

two years?

-What areas of my life will I focus on? Family, work, faith,

health, etc.?

-What are my strengths?

-What are my weaknesses?

-What will I improve?

-What should I learn about?

-What resources are available to help me reach my goals?

-How will I know I've accomplished my goals?

Identify things you've:

-Done well:

-Tried to do well:

-Done badly or not at all:

Write down your goals:

1.

2.

3.

4.

5.

6.

Now think about what it will take to accomplish them over a specific period of time. Take notes on such things as time commitments, costs, etc.

Review your goals every six months to stay on track.

Change your goals as your life changes.

Kim Manser Hofmann

E. "GOOD DAY" TO DO LIST

1.

2.

3.

4.

5.

6.

7.

8.

9.

10.

Kim Manser Hofmann

F. "BAD DAY" TO DO LIST

1.

2.

3.

4.

5.

6.

7.

8.

9.

10.

Kim Manser Hofmann

G. QUESTIONS TO ASK YOUR DOCTOR AND OTHER HEALTH ADVISORS

Why do I have aches and pains in the following locations? Describe the pain.

I've noticed the following patterns in pain I suffer; is there an explanation you can offer?

I have difficulty with the following daily living activities. Any suggestions?

What developments in research and alternative medicines should I be aware of?

Is there something else I should do to improve my daily living? Exercise, diet, alternative treatments, adaptive devices, etc?

Observations about emotional state (depressed, angry, frustrated, elated, etc.) For example, fill in the following blanks:

I feel _____ when I_____ because

_____.

Other questions/observations:

H. ADDITIONAL RESOURCES

American Academy
of Medical Acupuncture   www.medicalacupuncture.org

American Fibromyalgia
Syndrome Assoc., Inc.   www.afsafund.org

Arthritis Foundation (US)   www.arthritis.org

Association for Children
with Arthritis (Danish)   www.fnug.dk

Ehlers Danlos Support
Group (UK)   www.atv.ndirect.co.uk

European Lupus
Erythematosus Federation   www.elef.rheumanet.org

International League
Against Arthritis   www.ilar.org

Food and Nutrition
Information Center   www.nalusda.gov/fnic

International Osteoporosis
Foundation   www.effo.org

International Still's
Disease Foundation   www.stillsdisease.org

Johns Hopkins University Medical	www.intellihealth.com
Lupus Foundation of America	www.lupus.org
National Ankylosing Spondylitis Society (UK)	www.nass.co.uk
The Paget Foundation	www.paget.org
Psoriatic Arthropathy Alliance (UK)	www.paalliance.org
Raynaud's & Scleroderma Association (UK)	www.raynauds.demon.co.uk
Sjogren's Syndrome Foundation	www.sjogrens.com

I. SUGGESTIONS

This book is a combination of suggestions that I have for living effectively with arthritis. You may also have tips on easier living with arthritis. I look forward to hearing from you with your comments. Please e-mail suggestions and comments to kim@solutions4arthritis.com.

When you submit your thoughts and ideas, please include your own e-mail address and phone number. All submissions will become the property of Solutions for Arthritis (solutions4arthritis.com).

Kim Manser Hofmann

ABOUT THE AUTHOR

As a human resource consultant for over 20 years, Kim uses her innovative and strategic thinking to help arthritis patients cope with their disease. She has been an author, spokesperson and Arthritis Educator with the University of Texas Southwestern Medical Center at Dallas (UTSW) since 1992. Kim was diagnosed with rheumatoid arthritis in 1980. She credits the management of her disease to:
-excellent medical care
-proper diet, medication and exercise
-the love of her husband, children, family, friends and coworkers and
-her faith and positive attitude.

www.ingramcontent.com/pod-product-compliance
Lightning Source LLC
Chambersburg PA
CBHW020527290526
45786CB00002B/779